Alberta Ethnic German Politicians

Ernest G. Mardon, Ph. D

Austin A. Mardon, A.S.M., M.Sc.

Catherine Mardon

Edited by Pauline Balogun

Other Titles by Austin Mardon

International Law and Space Rescue Systems
Kensington Stone and Other Essays
Alone Against the Revolution
Political Networks in Alberta 1905-1992

Other Titles by Ernest Mardon

The Founding Faculty of the University of Lethbridge
Place Names of Southern Alberta
Who's Who in Federal Politics from Alberta Ridings
Community Names of Alberta

Collaborative Works by Austin & Ernest Mardon

Alberta Judicial Biographical Dictionary
Alberta Ethnic Mormon Politicians
Alberta Ethnic German Politicians
Alberta Mormon Politicians
Edmonton Political Biography
Alberta Political Biographical Dictionary
Alberta Executive Council 1905-1990
United Farmers of Alberta
Alberta Catholic Politicians
Alberta Anglican Politicians
What's in a Name?
Edmonton Members of the Legislature
Edmonton Municipal Politicians
Alberta Francophone Politicians

Alberta Ethnic German Politicians:

Alberta Political Candidates of German Ethnic Origin
Including
Winners and Losers in Territorial, Provincial, and Federal General Elections and Subsequent By-Elections:
1882-1990

Ernest G. Mardon, Ph. D.

Austin A. Mardon, A.S.M., M.Sc.

Catherine Mardon

Edited by Pauline Balogun

Golden Meteorite

Cover Design: Lawrence Dommer, 2011

Additional Copies can be ordered from:
Golden Meteorite Press
126 Kingsway Garden Post Office Box 34181, Edmonton, Alberta, CANADA. T5G 3G4

Library and Archives Canada Cataloguing in Publication

Mardon, Ernest G., 1928-
Alberta ethnic German politicians / Ernest G. Mardon, Austin A. Mardon, Catherine Mardon ; edited by Pauline Balogun.

Includes bibliographical references.
ISBN 978-1-897472-28-6

1. Politicians--Alberta--Biography. 2. Germans--Alberta-Politics and government--History. 3. Alberta--Politics and government--History.
I. Mardon, Austin A. (Austin Albert) II. Mardon, Catherine A., 1962-
III. Balogun, Pauline Jessica, 1994- IV. Title.

FC3700.G3M37 2011 971.23'0043100922 C2011-905439-6

Printed in Alberta.

Dedication

To Teresa May

E.G. & A.M.

To Quinn, my grandson

E.G.

Primary Sources:

The primary sources for factual data and biographical information are the Edmonton Bulletin, The Edmonton Journal, and The Calgary Herald, plus oral interviews conducted with living politicians during the past two years.

Acknowledgements:

To Susan Rauch, B.Ed. for typing this manuscript for us.

Table of Contents

PREFACE:

The following monograph covers ethnic German successful and unsuccessful federal, provincial, and territorial candidates from 1882 through to 1990. All successful and unsuccessful candidates' biographies were examined for membership in the German ethnic group. In some cases, the only ethnic link that exists that can be shown is the Germanic nature of the surname and/ or the Christian names.

We do not expect that we have included every ethnic German politician but we have examined every candidate in the soon to be published book Alberta Political Biographical Dictionary: 1882-1980. This larger work is being published under the auspices of Alberta Culture and Multiculturalism, Historic Resources Division.

The majority of information of the recent candidates biographical data has been acquired from pubic sources and supplemented by personal telephone interviews. Every attempt has been made to verify the information and confirm details from multiple sources.

The German ethnic is not one that is merely from what we currently envisage the nation state boundaries of the new unified Germany but encompasses those persons that held the major elements of the German culture in their lifestyle until they came to Canada.

The German ethnic group shares many of the same characteristics of political activism and participation, as we define it to be in putting oneself up to be elected as we see in other Albertans.

They have contributed to the great parliamentary system by their active participation in the political process. It is of interest that ethnic Germans were participating in a peaceful manner in the Democratic process in Canada during the Centuries earlier tumultuous times in Europe. This should be noted by the reader. Persons that are of German descent it should note have even served at the highest levels of the legislative system, the Speaker of the Alberta Provincial Legislature.

INTRODUCTION

By A. Mardon & E. Mardon

The first Ethnic Germans to arrive in what is Canada today were United Empire Loyalists who migrated from the newly formed United States of America into what remained British possessions in North America: the Lunnenburg Germans.

Alberta Ethnic German Politicians, 1880's – 1990's

"The Art of Biography

Is different from Geography:

Geography is about maps,

But Biography is about chaps."

G. K. Chesterton

WILLIAM ABERHART

Born December 30, 1878 on a farm near Seaforth, Huron County, Ontario, William Aberhart was the third son and fourth child of William Aberhart Sr., who had emigrated from Germany as a child, and Louisa Pepper. Educated at Seaforth, and Chatham

Business College, he attended Hamilton's Ontario Normal College, qualifying as a teacher in 1899. He taught two years at Wingham and nine at Brantford Central School, the last five as principal. In 1902, he married Jessie Flatt of Galt. In 1905, Aberhart seriously considered entering the Presbyterian ministry, but abandoned the idea for lack of financial support from the local presbytery. Between 1907 and 1911, he completed studies as an extra-mural student at Queen's University to earn a B. A. degree. In 1910 he moved his family to Calgary, where he became a principal of four schools in succession, the last Balmoral Heights (later Crescent Heights), where he remained from 1915 to 1935, gaining a reputation as an excellent teacher, an able administrator, and a firm disciplinarian.

By 1920, he was conducting Bible study classes and only five years later, he commenced broadcasting on CFCN radio, quickly becoming a well-known radio personality. By the early 1930's was reaching a radio audience estimated at 250,000 persons. In 1927, he opened up the Calgary Prophetic Bible Institute. In 1932, Aberhart became a strong radio advocate of Social Credit theory

Failing to interest Alberta's political parties, he organized a political movement based on masterful showmanship hundreds of study groups across the province similar to this Bible Study cells. The Social Credit movement ran a full slate of candidates, all hand□picked by Aberhart, in the 1935 provincial election, electing 56. He accepted the premiership and took the top-election rank into the Legislature. Once his efforts to introduce a Social Credit program were blocked in the courts, Aberhart settled down to give Albertans good government and withstand backbenchers' revolt over the failure to introduce Social Credit theories. He radically changed the educational system, introducing larger administrative units.

His administration was re-elected with a reduced majority in 1940. Claiming divine sanction for his party platform, "Bible Bill" capitalized on the discontent of the great depression to fashion a religious and political crusade for prosperity on the prairies. He died while still the Premier after a brief illness in Vancouver, May 23, 1943.

GERALD AMERONGEN

*See under GERALD JOSEP*H TAETS VON AMERONGEN.

MAXIMILLAN AMERONGEN

See under MAXMILLAN ERNEST BARON TAETS VON AMERONGEN

GEORGE R. AUSTIN

Interested in provincial politics, George R. Austin, running as a CCF candidate, unsuccessfully contested the five-member Calgary constituency in 1948. He placed nineteenth.

KARL BADKE

The name would indicate ethnic German descent. He was born in 1936. Coming to Albert in 1951, he settled in Edmonton. Since 1960, he has worked as a proprietor, accountant, controller, and financial officer for several companies. Interested in provincial politics, Karl Badke, running as the Representative Party's Candidate, unsuccessfully contested Edmonton Avonmore in 1986. He received 414 votes.

GEORGE BAUER

Interested in provincial politics, George Bauer, running as a Liberal, unsuccessfully contested Camrose in 1952.

JACK BERGEROU

Born in 1941. In the mid-1960's, he was a Fort McMurray bush pilot. Interested in Alberta politics, Jack Bergeron, running as a Progressive Conservative, unsuccessfully contested the August 20, 1968, Lac La Biche by-election. He placed second, losing to Social Crediter Dr. Damase David Bouvier by 1,527-vote margin. The vacancy occurred because of the resignation of the Alberta Liberal leader Michael Maccagno.

A. ERICH BIER

He was born April 7, 1943 at Grutz, Austria. Came to Albert a child in 1952, A. Erich Brier was educated at Coaldale and later at Victoria. As a young, he enlisted in the Princess Patricia's Canadian Light Infantry. After he served his term in the military, he settled in Edmonton and became a locksmith. A. Erich Bier unsuccessfully ran as the Reformed Party candidate for the Edmonton North Federal Riding in 1988.

ANDREW BLUM

The name would indicate ethnic German descent. He was born in 1944. He became a building contractor. Andrew Blum unsuccessfully ran as the Western Canada Concept candidate for the Smoky River Provincial Constituency in 1982.

THOMAS BOOKER

Interested in provincial politics, Thomas Booker, running as a Conservative candidate, unsuccessfully contested the Edson constituency in 1955.

W. F. BORGSTEDE

Interested in provincial politics, W. F. Borgstede, running as a Liberal, unsuccessfully contested Leduc in 1955.

HARVEY BOSSENBERRY

He served as an MLA.

HENRY (Hein) HEINRICH BR/EUTIGAM

Born in 1934 at Eifel, Germany where he lived until 1952 when he immigrated to Canada. He worked in construction for several years. He became the proprietor of a Calgary real estate company. Henry Brutigam unsuccessfully ran as a Western Canada Concept candidate for the Calgary Forest Lawn Provincial Constituency in 1982.

MICHAEL BRINGS

He was born in 1956, son to Gunther Brings, formerly of Dusseldorf, West Germany, and Rose Raufer, formerly of Heidelberg. His grand□father was a Dusseldorf alderman. Michael Brings unsuccessfully ran as a Liberal candidate for the Edmonton Avonmore Provincial Constituency in 1986.

DORIS S. BURGARDT

The name would indicate ethnic German descent. She

married Fred F. Burghardt. She was an active member of the New Democratic Party. Interested in federal politics, Doris S. Burghardt unsuccessfully contested the Edmonton Strathcona federal riding in the September 1984 general election. She placed second to Conservative incumbent David Kilgour with 17 percent.

ROBERT J. CRUMP

The name would indicate ethnic German descent. He was admitted to the Manitoba Bar in 1970. Coming to Alberta in 1973, he was admitted to the Bar. He became a Calgary lawyer. Robert J. Crump unsuccessfully ran as a Liberal for the Calgary Shaw Provincial constituency in 1989.

ELROY DEIMERT

He was born in 1953 at Lanigan, Saskatchewan, to Rev. R. E. Deimert. Educated at Calgary, he had experience in logging, farming, construction, and social work. Later he attended the University of Calgary, graduating with a Bachelor degree before he obtained a Masters degree at the University of Windsor. In the early 1980's, he was employed as an English instructor at the Grande Prairie Regional College. He was and active member of the New Democratic Party. Interested in federal politics, Elroy Deimert unsuccessfully contested the Peace River riding in the September 1984 general election. He placed second to conservative incumbent Albert Cooper with 15 percent of the vote. In 1984, Deimert was still an English instructor at the Grand Prairie Regional College.

ANN DORT-MACLEAN

See under ANN DORT- MACLEAN.

R. GERALD EHERER

The name would indicate ethnic German descent. He was admitted to the Alberta Bar in 1982. He became a Fairview lawyer. R. Gerald Eherer, unsuccessfully ran as a Liberal for the Dunvegan Provincial Constituency in 1989.

MARY LOU EHRENHOLZ

The name would indicate ethnic German descent. Interested in provincial politics, Mary Lou Ehrenholz, running as a Liberal, unsuccessfully contested Barrhead in 1986. She only received 664 votes. The Liberal candidate in the 1982 election, Nick Taylor obtained 3,330 votes.

PETER ENZENAUER

>>>>>>>>>

LAURIE FIEDLER

The name would indicate ethnic German descent. Born in 1959. In the mid-1980's, she was an "out of work" Lethbridge resident. Interested in provincial politics, Laurie Fiedler, running as a New Democratic, unsuccessfully contested Macleod in 1986. In a field of three candidates, he place last with only 12.4 percent of the votes cast.

BERNARD H. FRITZE

The name would indicate ethnic German descent. He

worked at the Red Deer Television station. Bernard H. Fritze unsuccessfully ran as a Liberal for the Red Deer North Provincial Constituency in 1989.

DANIEL FRITZE

The name would indicate ethnic German descent. As a young man, he enlisted in the Royal Canadian Mounted Police [RCMP]. He served twenty-five years with the force. He then became an Edmonton insurance claim adjustor. Daniel Fritze unsuccessfully ran as a Liberal for the Stony Plain Provincial Constituency in 1989.

MURRAY FUHR

The name would indicate ethnic German descent. He was a candidate in the 1982 election.

JOHN JOST GicETZ

Born June 6, 1859 at Brand Bank, Newfoundland, son of

Thomas Gtz and Catherine Jost. His ancestors came to Canada form Germany in 1750. Educated at Mount Allison University and settled at Guysboror, Nova Scotia. Came to Alberta with his mother in 1885, they homesteaded in the Balmoral district near Red Deer. They were the first settlers in the district. Gtz, who was a nephew of Dr. Leonard Gaetz, was active in community affairs, helping to establish the Balmoral school. When the University of Alberta was created, he was appointed a member of the University Senate. Interested in provincial politics, John Jost Gtz, running as a Liberal, successfully contested the 1917 Red Deer, by-election. He sat in the Legislature for four years as a private member on the government side of the house. He was defeated in his re-election bid in 1927. Gaetz donated a portion of his land to the Methodist Church for a graveyard, now Red Deer cemetery and established Gaetz Lake Sanctuary. In 1905, he married Grace Elder of Seaforth, Ontario. He was a Methodist. He died on December 24, 1937 at the age of seventy-nine.

LEO GAETZ

Born June 7, 1841 at Musqudoboit Harbor, Nova Scotia, son

of Leonard Gaetz and Catherine Ritzy. His father was a farmer, miller and operated a small trading vessel. The Gaetz had originally come from Saxony, Prussia in the 18th Century and had settled in Lunnenburg. At the age of 19 he commenced preaching. After he was ordained a Methodist Preacher, he served congregations at Middle Musquaodoboit, Picton, Nova Scotia, and Fredrickton, New Brunswick. In 1876 he was transferred to St. James, Montreal, the largest Methodist Church in Canada. He also was pastor at Hamilton and London, Ontario. Due to illness, he was forced to give up the active ministry. He came to Alberta in 1883 to homestead in the Red Deer Valley. He was the first pioneer in the district. His wife and 11 children joined him the next year. He became a prosperous farmer and established a trading post on the Red Deer River. The Calgary to Edmonton trail reached his farm in 1890, and the community of Red Deer grew upon his land. He was Red Deer's first Postmaster. In 1895, he returned to the active ministry, spending five years in Brandon, and then another five years in the Wesley Church, Winnipeg. Always interested in politics, he spoke at the Halifax celebration connected with Confederation in 1867. He was a friend of Prime Minister John A. Macdonald. In 1888 the

Prime Minister offerred him the vacancy seat in the Senate, caused by the death of Senator Richard Hardisty. Gaetz declined and the appointment went to James Loughheed, a young Calgary lawyer. A conservative, Leo Gaetz unsuccessfully contested Red Deer in 1905, defeated by Liberal candidate, John T. Moore. He died June 6, 1907 in Red Deer at the age of sixty-six.

KURT GEBAUER

Born in 1928 in Germany. he attended Hamburg University for a year, studying pre-medicine. Came to Canada in 1955, he settled in Calgary where he is a chemical laboratory technician on the University Campus. Interested in provincial politics, Kurt Gebauer, running as a New Democrat candidate, unsuccessfully contested Calgary East in 1967. During the campaign, he maintained that university education should be free.

FREDRICK WILLIAM GERSHAW

Born April 11, 1883 at Emerson, Manitoba, son of Theodore Gershaw and Margaret Clark. His father was of German descent. Educated at Emerson, he attended the University of Manitoba, graduating in Medicine. Came to Alberta in 1906, he settled at Medicine Hat where he was a prominent physician and surgeon for the next forty years. Active in Civic affairs, he served twelve years on the Medicine hat School Board. Interested in federal politics, Dr. Fredrick William Gershaw, running as a Liberal, unsuccessfully contested the Medicine Hat riding in the December 1921 general election. He was defeated by the United Farmers of Alberta [UFA] incumbent Robert Gardiner who had won the June 1921 federal by-election. In the 1925 federal election, Dr. Gershaw was elected and held the seat for the next twenty-five years except for the 1935 to 1940 period when it was held by the Social Credit. He was re-□elected in the 1926, 1930, and 1940 federal elections. Prime Minister Mackenzie King appointed Dr. Gershaw to the Senate in April 1945. He sat in the Red Chamber as an Alberta Senator for the next twenty-three years. In 1912 he married Harriet Grace Clarke of Ninga, maitoba. They had four daughters. He died on June 25, 1968 in Ottawa at the age of eighty-five.

WILLIAM A. GRIESBACH

MLA; MP; Sen.>>>>

ERIKA GUIDERA

She was born in 1929 at Braunau, Austria, daughter of Micahel Mitterbauer and Christensi Sielzehnriiebl. After the war, she moved to Scotland where she trained as a nurse. Came to Alberta in 1955, she settled at Edmonton where she became involved in the medical field as a medical secretary. She married Joseph Guidera. They have four children. Erika Guidera unsuccessfully ran for the Edmonton Whitemud in 1982 and again for the Edmonton South Federal Riding in 1984.

HERMAN HAUCH

Born in Saxony, Germany, son of Max Hauch. Came to Alberta in 1923, young Hauch assisted his uncle Gus Hauch in clearing land on his homestead in the Freedom district,near Barrhead. In time he became a well-known farmer in his own right, and a director of Alberta Poultry Marketeers. In 1950, Herman Hauch married Mrs. Elizabeth Lemmel, a widow from Northeast Germany, who had two children. Interested in provincial politics,

Herman Hauch, running as the NDP candidate, unsuccessfully contested Pembina in 1963. In a field of five candidates, he placed last. In the fall of 1963, Hauch retired from farming and moved to Barrhead to live. An Elizabeth Hauch was listed in the telephone book at 674-2525.

RUDOLPH HENNIG

>>>>>>

WARREN HENDRICKSON

He worked as a businessman in Fort Saskatchewan and took an interest in politics. Warren Hendrickson ran unsuccessfully as a Confederation of Regions candidate in the federal Elk Island riding during the 1988 election.

SAMUIL HERMAN

Born December 31, 1928 on a farm near Duvall, Saskatchewan, son of Jacob Herman (1897-1981), formerly a Russian residing on the Volga, and Maria Kallen (1900-1981). Both his parents, who were Lutherans, fled from Russia during the political disturbances of 1905. He became a financial planner in Lloydminster. Sam Herman unsuccessfully ran as a Liberal candidate for the Lloydminster/Cutbank Saskatchewan provincial Constituency in 1975. He came to Alberta in 1977, he settled at Lloydminster. Sam Herman ran unsuccessfully as a Reform Party candidate in the Federal Vegreville Riding during the 1988 election.

DANIEL P. HERMANSEN

He resided in Edmonton. Daniel P. Hermansen ran unsuccessfully as an Independent candidate in the federal Edmonton Strathcona riding during the 1988 election.

MICHAEL HERMANSEN

He became a professional engineer, residing in Westerose. He ran unsuccessfully as a Western Independence Party Candidate in the federal Wetaskiwin riding during the 1988 election.

CORNELIUS HIEBERT

Born August 2, 1862 in a Mennonite colony in Southern Russia, near the shore of the Sea of Azov. He came to Canada as a child with his parents, who settled at Steinbeck, Manitoba. When he became twenty-one, he left the colony and in time became a successful merchant at Altona. Came to Alberta in 1890, he settled in Didsbury. He became a prominent merchant. There were many other Mennonites in the District. Interested in provincial politics, Cornelius Hiebert, running as a Conservative, successfully contested Rosebud in 1905. He sat in the legislature for four years. In 1909, he failed in his re-election bid. Hiebert was one of the two Conservatives in the first Legislature. The main local issue in 1905 was that the Liberal administration of Rutherford would not permit the Mennonites to establish their own separate school. Hiebert also was a strong prohibitionist. Hiebert failed in his effort to make Banff, the scenic Rocky Mountain community, the site of the new Provincial capital. He died March 20, 1919 at the age of fifty-six.

VERN HOFF

The name would indicate ethnic German descent. Vern Hoff unsuccessfully ran as a Western Canada candidate for the

Drumheller Provincial Constituency in 1982.

SIGMUND KEHLERT

Born Febraury 6, 1922 at Lamont Alberta, son of William Kehlert. His ancestors were German who entered Russian in the time of Peter the Great. When his grandfather was killed by Russian cossacks in 1890, the family returned to Germany. He quit school in grade nine to work on the family farm. In 1976, he left the farm to become an agricultural implement dealer. Sigmund Kehlert ran unsuccessfully as a Confederation of Regions candidate in the federal Edmonton North riding during the 1988 election. During the campaign, he stated that he was in favor of capital punishment.

WILLY KELCH

The name would indicate ethnic German descent. Born and raised in West Germany. Came to Albert in 1953, he settled at Calgary where he worked in the construction industry. In 1977, he became a Czar rancher. Interested in Provincial politics, Willy Kelch, running as a New Democratic Party candidate unsuccessfully contested Wainwright in 1986. He placed second, losing to Conservative incumbent Robert Fischer by a 3,138 vote margin. He also unsuccessfully ran as the New Democratic Party candidate for the Wainwright Provincial Constituency in 1989.

HERMAN KLEEN

Born in 1950, Herman Kleen was educated in Edmonton. He became a psychiatric nurse at the Edmonton royal Alexander Hospital. Herman Kleen ran unsuccessfully as a Rhinoceros candidate in the federal St. Albert riding during the 1988 election.

JOHN KLOSTER

Born in 1927 in Saskatchewan. He attended the University of Ottawa, graduating in arts. He then came to Alberta where he attended the University of Alberta in Edmonton where he obtained an education degree. Kloster taught in Edmonton for the next twenty years. Interested in provincial politics, John Kloster, running as a Liberal, unsuccessfully contested the new constituencies of Strathcona South in 1967. In a field of four candidates, he placed last and forfeited his deposit.

HENRY MENDELBAUM

Born in 1947 in Poland, came to Canada as a child, his family settled in Winnipeg. During the 1970's, he worked as a ministerial assistant for the NDP government of Manitoba and was part of a special research group studying rural economic development in the province. Came to Alberta in 1979, he settled in Edmonton where he became a research consultant. Interested in federal politics, Henry Mendelbaum, running as the NDP candidate, unsuccessfully contested the Vegreville riding in the 1980 general election. In a field of six candidates, he placed third. Of the 34,000 votes cast, he won 3,172.

GARY KUMP

The name would indicate ethnic German descent. He became an Edmonton resident. Active in Community affairs, he served as vice president of the Edmonton Federation of Community Leagues. Gary Kump unsuccessfully ran as a Progressive Conservative for the Edmonton Beverley Provincial Constituency in 1989.

HARRY KUNTZ

The name would suggest ethnic German descent. Harry Kuntz was born in 1929. Active in Community affairs, Kuntz served as a Camrose alderman in the 1960's. He was also a prominent Camrose businessman. Kuntz was President of a seismic drilling company and the owner of a 2,000-acre farm in the Winburn district. Active in community affairs, he served as Mayor of Camrose. Interested in federal politics, Harry Kuntz, running as a Progressive Conservative successfully contested the Battle River riding in the 1972 general election. He had more than a 12,000-vote majority over his nearest rival Vincent Ericksson, the New Democratic Party candidate. He sat in parliament for only one year as a private member on the opposition benches. He died November 16, 1973 at Ottawa at the age of forty-four while still a sitting member.

KURRI LANTERMAN

The name would indicate ethnic German descent. She was the daughter of Don Lanterman who worked in the oil field transportation business. She was still a student when she became active in politics. Kurri Lanterman unsuccessfully ran as an Independent for the Red Deer North Provincial constituency in 1989.

KAREN LEIBOVICI

The name would indicate ethnic German descent. Born in 1953 at Edmonton. Educated at Edmonton, she then received business, labor, and social service experience. Interested in provincial politics, Karen Leibovici, running as a Liberal, unsuccessfully contested Edmonton Jasper Place in 1986. In a field of three candidates, she placed third with a respectable twenty percent of the vote. During the campaign, Ms. Leibovici declared that if elected, she would adopt an ongoing consultative approach. Residents' frustrations over the arrogant and silent response to their concerns would be addressed by her open-door policy. She became a labor relations officer with the City of Edmonton. Karen Leibovici unsuccessfully ran as a Liberal for the Edmonton Jasper Place provincial constituency in 1989.

ANN DORT- MACLEAN

The name would indicate ethnic German descent. Interested in federal politics, Ann Dort-Maclean, running as the NDP candidate, unsuccessfully contested the Athabasca riding in the September 1984 general election. She place second to Conservative incumbent Jack Shields with 17 percent of the vote. Interested in provincial politics, Ann Dort-MacLean, running as a New Democrat, unsuccessfully contested the Fort McMurray constituency in 1986. She placed second, loosing to Conservative incumbent 'Norm' Norman Weiss by a 698 vote margin.

DAVID WILLIAN MTCHE

David Mtche was born on May 29, 1929 in Olds, Alberta, the son of Fredrick Mtche and Emile Reule. His ancestors were German although his mother was born in South Dakota. He attended Cascade College, Portland, Oregon as a mature student. He farmed for most of his life. Due to an automobile accident, he became physically handicapped. The Provincial Correction Services employed him. David William Mtche unsuccessfully ran as the Western Canada Concept candidate for the Edmonton Highlands Provincial Constituency in 1982.

GUS MALCHOW

Born in 1856 at Stettin Germany, the son of a sea captain, Gus Malchow served for four years with the Prussian Cavalry before immigrating to the United States in 1880. He became a farmer in the Fairmont District of Nebraska. In 1882, he married Antoria Roesler, an Austrian. They had twelve children. Drought caused Malchow to move north to Minnesota, from where he came to Alberta in 1901, homesteading near Ponoka. Eight years later, he moved to Stavely where he became a prosperous farmer. Interested in provincial politics, Malchow unsuccessfully contested Claresholm in 1913. In 1930, he was elected Mayor of Stavely. He died in October of 1933.

VERN MEEK

The name would indicate ethnic German descent. He became a Three Hills hog farmer. Vern Meek unsuccessfully ran as a Western Canada Concept candidate for the Three Hills Provincial constituency in 1982.

FRED MERTZ

The name would indicate possible ethnic German descent although because he was born in Hungary, there is the possibility that it is a Hungarian surname. He came to Canada with his parents as an infant in 1956. Fred Mertz was educated at Redwater. He became a large poultry farmer east of Calgary. He also is completing a Certified Public Accountants course in 1989. Fred Mertz, unsuccessfully ran as the New Democratic Party candidate for the Three Hills Party constituency in 1989.

THORA MIESSNER

The name would indicate ethnic German descent. She attended the University of Saskatchewan in Saskatoon graduating in education in 1965. Came to Alberta, she settled in Calgary where she taught. Interested in provincial politics, Thora Miessner, running as a New Democrat, unsuccessfully contested Calgary Elbow in 1982 and then unsuccessfully contested Calgary Foothills in 1986. She placed second in Calgary Foothills to Conservative incumbent

Janet Koper by a 3,445-vote margin. In 1989, she was a Calgary schoolteacher.

EMMETT GEORGE MOHLER

Emmett was born August 9, 1902 near Sioux City, Iowa, the son of Frank Mohler and Mary Murphy. He came to the District of Alberta, NWT in 1903, as an infant, his father homesteaded in the Rolling Hills District. Educated at Rolling Hills and Camrose, he attended the Camrose Normal School, qualifying as a teacher. He taught briefly and then worked in his father's construction company. In 1933, he commenced farming. He specialized in seed growing. He was a prominent Camrose farmer for thirty years. Active in community affairs, he served on the Camrose Town Council for five years. Interested in provincial politics, Emmett Mohler, running as a Progressive Conservative unsuccessfully contested Camrose in 1967. He ran second to Social Credit incumbent Chester Sayers.

REINHARD MUELLER

An Edmonton resident, he was employed as an engineering technician. Interested in Federal politics, Reinhard Mueller, running as a Social Crediter, unsuccessfully contested the Edmonton South riding in the September 1984 general election. In a field of seven candidates, he placed last.

MARTIN NAUNDORF

The name would indicate ethnic German descent. He was a St. Paul resident in 1986. Because of his interest in politics, Martin Naundorf, running as a New Democrat, contested St. Paul in 1986 although unsuccessfully. He received 22% of the votes cast.

BRADLEY NEUBAUER

The name would indicate ethnic German descent. Born in 1962 at Medicine Hat and raised on an Irvine farm. He attended the University of Calgary. While still a student, he became active in politics. Brad Neubauer unsuccessfully ran as the New Democrat candidate for the Bow Valley Provincial constituency in 1982.

CHARLES HERMAN OLIN

MLA>>>>>>>>

CONNIE OSTERMAN

The name would indicate ethnic German descent. She was born in 1937 at Acme, Alberta. She farmed with her husband in the Vulcan district before moving to Carstairs in 1958. The Ostermans became well-known Carstairs farmers. Interested in Provincial politics, Connie Osterman, running as a Progressive Conservative successfully contested Three Hills in 1979. She was re-elected in 1982 and 1986. In 1979, she was appointed the government whip in the Legislature. In 1982, Premier Lougheed named her to the Cabinet as Minister of Consumer and Corporate Affairs. In February 1986, Premier Getty transferred Mrs. Osterman to the Social Services and Community Health portfolio.

FREDRICK G. PAASCHE

The name would indicate ethnic German descent. Fredrick G. Paasche unsuccessfully ran as a Liberal for the Vegreville Provincial constituency in 1989.

MICHAEL PAWLUS

Michael Pawlus was born in 1924. During World War II, he survived four years inside a German concentration camp. He finally escaped in 1945 and commenced working for the American army. By the 1980's, he was a well-known Edmonton engineer-businessman. In January 1985, Palus became the leader of the `right-wing' Heritage Party. In the February 21, 1985 Spirit River/ Fairview by-election, Pawlus placed last in a field of seven candidates. In the May 8, 1986 Alberta election, Michael Pawlus unsuccessfully contested the Edmonton Mill Woods constituency. He only received 132 votes although none of the other five `Heritage' candidates did well at the polls.

DENNIS JOHN PETER

Born October 12, 1939 at Bawlf, Alberta, son of Joseph Peter, formerly of Odessa, Russia and Matilda Urlacher. Both his parents were of German descent. He became an automotive instructor at Northern Alberta Institute of Technology [NAIT]. Dennis John Peter unsuccessfully ran as the Western Canada Concept Candidate for the Edmonton Belmont Provincial Constituency in 1982.

DARRELL W. PIEHL

He was a resident of Fort Macleod. Darrell W. Piehl unsuccessfully ran as a Liberal for the Macleod Provincial constituency in 1989.

JURGEN PREUGSCHAS

The first name and surname would strongly suggest ethnic German descent. Jurgen Preugschas unsuccessfully ran as a Liberal for the Whitecourt Provincial constituency in 1989.

RAYMOND RECKSEIDLER

The name would suggest ethnic German descent. Interested in provincial politics, Raymond Reckseidler ran was an Independent in 1975 then as the Representative Party's candidate, unsuccessfully contesting the Innisfail constituency in 1986.

CARL REIMER

She was born in 1956 in Alberta. A Calgary resident, she is a qualified nurse who is studying for her Masters degree in health care research. Interested in provincial politics, Carl Reimer, running as a Liberal unsuccessfully contested Calgary McKnight in 1986.

DAVID J. REIMER

He was born in Steinbach, Manitoba, son of Mennonites Rev John K. Reimer and Liona Reinmer. His grandparents came from Prussia in the 19th century and were pioneer settlers in southern Manitoba. As a young man, he became a shoe salesman in Winnipeg. In 1972, he opened his own clothing store in Steinbach. He was the proprietor for eight years. He married Catherine [Katy] Unrk daughter of former residents of the Soviet Union. Came to Alberta in 1980, he became Mennonite minister at Wetaskiwin. Rev. David J. Reimer unsuccessfully ran as the Christian heritage Party candidate for the Wetaskiwin Federal Riding in 1988.

MARTIN ROBERT

Born in Germany. He was active in the trade union movement. Came to Alberta in the 1970's, he settled in Edmonton where he joined the Communist party and became active in civic politics and the peace movement. Martin Robert unsuccessfully ran as a Communist for the Edmonton Calder Provincial Constituency in 1986. He received 26 votes.

A. S. de ROSENRALL

>>>>>>>>>>>>

BERNARD SAWATZKY

Bernard was born September 20, 1932 on a Prince Albert homestead. He was of German descent. His grandparents left Russia in the 1880's after being in that country for one hundred years. His father Abram Sawatzky was born in Saskatchewan and his mother, Suzy Harder, was a Dutch women. Came to Alberta in 1954, he qualified as a carpenter. He worked for an Edmonton contractor. He married Mary Yaroslwsky, a Ukranian Albertan. Bernard Sawtzky ran unsuccessfully as a western Independence Party candidate in the Federal Edmonton East riding during the 1988 election.

MURRAY WILLIAM SCAMBLER

Born in April 21, 1954 at Edmonton. His father was Charles Scambler of Winnipeg and Thelma Parry, formerly of Regina. He became the proprietor of a Small Edmonton business. He failed to be elected as an Edmonton alderman in 1983. He unsuccessfully ran as an Alberta Reform Movement for the Edmonton Strathcona Provincial Constituency in 1982. Murray Scambler unsuccessfully ran as a Liberal for the Edmonton Millwoods Provincial Constituency in 1989.

RUDOLPH SCHEMPP

The name would indicate ethnic German descent. He was born in the Ukraine. He came from West Germany to Canada in 1954 and became a resident of Redcliff. He operated a farm and barbershop. He ran unsuccessfully as the New Democratic Party Candidate for the Cypress Provincial Constituency in 1982 and again in 1989.

BRANNY SCHEPANOVICH

The name would indicate ethnic German descent. He was born in 1941 in Cadomin. Educated at Edson, he attended the University of Alberta, graduating from the faculty of Arts in1963 and in Law in1967. While on campus, he was president of the Student Union (1966-1967) and was an active member of the Liberal Club. He also served as editor of The Gateway, the student newspaper. Schepanovich gained admittance to the Alberta Bar in 1968. That year he worked as an Action Trudeau coordinator during the federal election campaign that resulted in the Liberals winning four seats in Alberta. Schepanovich then practiced law in Edmonton. Interested in federal politics, Branny Schepanovich unsuccessfully contested the Edmonton Centre riding twice: first in the 1972 general election and again in the 1974 general election. On both occasions, he placed second, losing to Tory Steve Paproski. He continued to practice law until his death on January 15 in 2007.

THOMAS SCHEPENS

Born in 1952 and raised in Winnipeg, Manitoba. He attended the University where he studied political science and law. Later he became a police officer. Coming to Alberta in 1976, he settled in

Calgary where he became an investment stockbroker. Tom Schepens, running as a New Democrat, unsuccessfully contested Calgary North West in 1986. He placed second, losing to Conservative Dr. Stan Cassin by a 4,398-vote margin and forfeited his deposit. He ran unsuccessfully as a New Democrat in the federal Calgary North riding in the 1988 election.

LAWRENCE SCHLAMP

He was born June 25, 1925 in Winnipeg, to Fred and Katherine Schlamp. During World War II, he enlisted in the Royal Canadian Navy and served on the H. M. C. S. "Ontario" in the North Atlantic. After the War, he operated the family farm. Lawrence Paul 'Larry' Schlamp unsuccessfully ran as a Social Crediter for the Springfield [Manitoba] Federal Riding in 1957 and for the Lac de Bonney Provincial Constituency in 1959. Came to Alberta in 1958, he first worked as a barber and then operated two trucks servicing oil wells. Lawrence Paul Schlamp unsuccessfully ran as a Confederation of Regions candidate for the Vegreville Federal Riding in 1984 and again in 1988.

DALE SCHLENKER

The name would indicate German descent. Born in 1955 at Botha, Alberta, he was raised on a farm. Educated at Stettler, he then became a civic employee of the City of Red Deer. In 1973 he attended Hillcrest Christian College for a semester before enrolling in the Calgary Bureau Bible College. When he was sixteen, he became active in the Social Credit League and two years later elected onto the provincial executive. Interested in federal politics, 19 year old Dale Schlenker unsuccessfully contested the Calgary North riding in the 1974 general election. He received 1,354 of the 46,000 votes cast. Tory veteran Eldon Woolliams retained the seat.

JAMES B. SCHLEPPE

Born in 1946 at Calgary and raised on a Beiseker farm. He attended the University of Calgary, graduating in education in 1972. He taught school at Fort Vermillion and Calgary before studying theology in Ottawa. He became a Beiseker resident. James B. Schleppe unsuccessfully ran as a New Democratic Party Candidate for the Tree Hills Provincial Constituency in 1982.

MATTHEW SCHMALTZ, SR.

Born in 1891 near Odessa, Russia, son of Ludwig Schmaltz and Juliana Vatter, he was a descendent of a German-speaking Lorraine family who had moved there in 1808. The family moved to North Dakota when he was an infant and he was educated in the United States. Came to Alberta in 1908, he homesteaded near Beiserker. He became a prominent farmer. Active in community affairs, he served for years on the Norquay Municipal Council. For a time he was reeve. Interested in provincial politics, Matthew Schmaltz, running as an Independent, unsuccessfully contested Didsbury in 1948. He lost his deposit in the election that returned Social Credit incumbent Howard Hammell. In 1960, he retired to Beiserker.

HORST ADOLPH LOUIS SCHMID

Born April 29, 1933 at Munich, German, and son of Karl A. Schmid came to Canada as a young man, he studied Grade XII after his arrival. By the early 1970's, he was an Edmonton businessman connected with the export trade. Interested in provincial politics Horst Schmid, running as a Progressive Conservative, successfully contested Edmonton Avonmore in 1971. He sat in the legislative for fifteen years. Premier Louheed appointed Horst Schmid Minister of Culture, Youth and Recreation in 1971. He held the culture portfolio for eight years. From 1979 to 1982, he was Minister of State for International trade. In 1986, he placed second, losing to Marie Laing of the NDP by a 93-vote margin.

KEITH SCHMIDT

He was admitted to the Alberta Bar in 1979. Keith Schmidt became a Camrose lawyer. He unsuccessfully ran as a Western Canada Concept candidate for the Camrose provincial Constituency.

RAY E. SCHMIDT

He was a Blackfalds farmer. Interested in provincial politics, Ray E. Schmidt, running as the CCF candidate, twice unsuccessfully contested Rocky Mountain House. He ran first in 1948 and then again in 1959. On both occasions, veteran Social

Credit candidate, Alfred Hooke, won the seat.

WERNER G. SCHMIDT

Born in 1932 at Cooldate, Alberta, and raised on a farm. His family was an active member of the Mennonite Brethorn Church. Educated at Coaldale, he attended the University of Alberta in Edmonton, graduating in education. Schmidt then taught school at Lethbridge before becoming the principal of the Crooked Creek centralized school. In 1968, he returned to the University of Alberta to study for his doctoral degree in education administration. While on campus, he served on the Board of Governors as a graduate student representative. At the same time, he worked as the executive director of the Alberta School Trustees Association in its Edmonton Head Office. He was a member of the advisory Committee that recommended changes in the School Act. Interested in provincial politics, Werner Schmidt, running as a Social Creditor, unsuccessfully contested Edmonton in 1971. He placed second, losing to Conservative Educator Dr. Bert Hohol. Later he became a vice president of Lethbridge Community College. On the resignation of Harry E. Strom, Werner Schmidt was named the Alberta Social Credit leader. In the 1975 Alberta election, Schmidt unsuccessfully contested Taber/Warner. He placed second, losing to Progressive Conservative Bob Bogle.

HAROLD SCHNEIDER

His name would indicate that he was of ethnic German descent. The record shows that he was interested in provincial politics. Harold Schneider, running as the Representative Party candidate, unsuccessfully contested Wetaskiwin/ Leduc in 1986.

PETER SCHNEIDER

The name would indicate ethnic German descent. He became a supervisor with Alberta Government Telephones. He ran as a Liberal candidate in the Provincial Edmonton Strathcona Constituency in the 1986 election.

CURTIS SCHCEP

Born October 16, 1957 at Fairview, Alberta, the son of Lester Schoepp. His father came to Alberta from Germany early in the century, and his mother, Lotta Huppie, was of Metis descent from the Lac La Biche area. He married Leane Miller. They have three children. He studies music at Edmonton's Grant MacEwan College. A financial institution employed him. Curtis Schoepp ran unsuccessfully as a Confederation of Regions Candidate in the Federal St. Albert riding during the 1988 election.

ELZIEN SCHOPMAN

He was a Little Bow farmer. Elzien Schopman unsuccessfully ran as a Liberal for the Little Bow Provincial Constituency in 1989.

KEITH SCHULTZ

The name would indicate ethnic German descent. He became an Edmonton automobile salesman. Keith Schultz unsuccessfully ran as a Social Crediter for the Edmonton Whitemud Provincial constituency in 1982.

DORIS SCHUPP

Doris Schupp unsuccessfully ran as a Communist for the

Calgary Millican Provincial Constituency in 1982.

ERNEST 'ERNIE' J. SEHN

He served as the Lac La Biche Director of Human Services Programs. Ernest J. Sehn unsuccessfully ran as Liberal for the Beaver River Federal Riding in 1988. In 1989 there was a telephone listing for Sehn.

GEORGE WILBERT SMITH

Born April 24, 1855 at Maitland, Nova Scotia, son of Morris Smith and Ann Gaetz. His father was English while his mother was German, a relation of Rev. Leo Gaetz. Educated at Maitland, he qualified as a teacher. He taught in the Maritimes for a number of years. Came to Alberta in 1883, Smith was an early pioneer of the Red Deer district. He also was the first schoolteacher in Central Alberta. He taught for a number of years before going into business. Smith played an active role in the development of Red Deer. Active in civic affairs, he served for a number of years on the town council before being elected the Mayor in 1917. He was also chairman of the school board.

He became a prominent businessman. He was president of Smith Land Company and a director of Western General Electric. Interested in provincial politics, G. W. Smith,running as the United Farmers of Alberta candidate successfully contested Red Deer constituency in 1921. Smith sat in the Legislature until the time of his death. he was married to the eldest daughter of Rev. Leo Gaetz, pioneer Methodist missionary and founder of Red Deer.

They had four sons and four daughters. One daughter married James G. La France and another Edgar G. Jones. He died on August 1, 1931 in Red Deer at the age of seventy-six.

DOUGLAS SNIDER

The name would indicate ethnic German descent. Douglas Snider unsuccessfully ran as a Progressive Conservative for the Spirit River/Fairview Provincial constituency in 1982.

LEONARD STAHL

Born in 1930 at Alcomdale. He attended the Three Hills Praire Bible Institute and continued his theological studies in

Vancouver. In 1954 he was ordained a Pentacostal clergyman. Later he settled in Edmonton and became a public relations consultant. Interested in provincial politics, Leonard Stahl, running as a Liberal, unsuccessfully contested Edmonton Centre in 1971.

JOESEPH EMMETT STAUFFER

MLA>>>>>>

ROBERT E. SWEIGARD

Born in 1962, son of Ken and Audrey Sweigard. He qualified as an accountant. Interested in federal politics, Robert Sweigard, running as a Social Credit, unsuccessfully contested the Peace River riding in the September 1984 general election. In a field of six, he placed last and forfeited his deposit. In 1987 he was living in Grand Prairie, employed as an accountant.

HANS VISSER

He became a Medicine Hat agri-business man. Hans Visser ran unsuccessfully as a Christian Heritage Party candidate in the Medicine Hat federal riding during the 1988 election.

GERALD JOSEPH TAETS VON AMERONGEN

Born July 18, 1914 at Winnipeg, son of Maximilion W.E. Taets V. Amerongen and Maria Waas. He attended school in Regina, Saskatoon and Edmonton. He attended the University of Alberta, graduating in arts and then in law in 1944. While he was on campus, he was president of the Students Union. he was admitted to the Alberta Bar in 1946. He then became an Edmonton lawyer. He was created a Q. C. in 1967. In 1943 he had married Elizabeth Helen Fethersonhouse. they had eight children. Active in community affairs, he served on the Misericordia and General Hospital Boards for many years. Gerald Amerongen, running as a Progressive Conservative, unsuccessfully contested the Edmonton Provincial constituencies in 1955, 1959, 1963, and 1967. He was first elected to the Legislature in 1971. he sat for fifteen years in the house as speaker of the Alberta Legislative Assembly. In 1986, he was not re-elected and so returned to his Edmonton law practice.

MAXMILLAN ERNEST BARON TAETS VON AMERONGEN

Born in 1875 in Bessungen, Hesse, Germany into a family of

Old Netherlands nobility, and educated at Darmstadt, Maximilian Ernest Baron Taets von Amerongen converted to Catholicism as a youth. After two years in London, he settled in Manitoba, in 1905 and became a British subject in 1910. He had intended to enlist in the Royal North West Mounted Police, but instead joined the Oblate fathers. He taught at Lebret, Saskatchewan, as a scholastic, but later left the Order. He took a leading part in Catholic and German affairs in western Canada for many years. Arriving in Alberta in 1928, he became a successful Edmonton businessman. A life-long Conservative, Amerongen unsuccessfully contested the Leduc constituency in the 1935 provincial election. In 1965, Pope Paul II awarded him the papal medal "Proecclesia et Pontifice" for his work connected with Edmonton's St. Joseph Cathedral and the Legion of Mary. He died November 20, 1968 in Edmonton.

JOSEPH ALBERT WANNER

Born September 3, 1919 at Gravelock, Saskatchewan, to a Jacob Wanner, formerly of Odessa, Russia. His ancestors were Germans who moved into Russia at the invitation of Empress Catherine the Great in the 17th Century. During World War II, he served with the South Saskatchewan Regiment. After the war, he was the proprietor of an Edmonton sporting goods store as well as a real estate agent. Joseph Albert Wanner unsuccessfully ran as a Western Canada Concept candidate for the Edmonton Gold Bar Provincial constituency in 1982. Joseph Albert Wanner died May 5, 1986 at Edmonton, Alberta.

JOHN S. WEBB

The name would suggest ethnic German descent. He was born in 1942. He was admitted to the Alberta Bar in 1973. He then served as a Calgary crown prosecutor. Later he became a Calgary criminal lawyer. John S. Webb unsuccessfully ran as a Liberal for the Calgary Elbow Provincial constituency in 1982.

GORDON E. WEESE

Born in 1932. He attended the University of Toronto. When he came to Alberta as a young man, he taught in rural schools before becoming an instructor at Edmonton's Alberta College. For several years, he was secretary of the Christian Movement. In 1966, he commenced doing graduate studies while being a teaching assistant at the University of Alberta. Interested in provincial politics, Gordon Weese, running as the NDP candidate, unsuccessfully contested Strathcona Centre in 1967. In a field of four candidates, he placed last and forfeited his deposit. The seat was retained by Social Credit Health Minister Dr. J. Donovan Ross.

CONRAD WEIDHAMMER

MLA>>>>

ROY JOSEPH WEIDEMANN

The name would indicate ethnic German descent. He was admitted to the Alberta Bar in 1960. He became a Medicine Hat Lawyer. Roy J. Weidemann unsuccessfully ran as a Liberal for the Medicine Hat Provincial constituency in 1967.

CONRAD WEIDENHAMMER

Born January 27, 1866 near St. Clemon, Wesley township, Ontario,son of Christopher Weidenhammer and Annie Brodbeck, both of whom had been born in Germany. Educated at Elmira, Ontario. He farmed in Ontario and served five years as a school trustee. For a long time he was a president of an Ontario Cheese factory. Came to Alberta, he became a prosperous Spruce Grove farmer. He served eleven years as a school trustee in Alberta. A Conservative, he contested unsuccessfully Stony Plain in 1905. He was elected for Stony Plain in 1913, defeating Liberal incumbent, J. A. McPherson. He sat until he retired in 1917.

'NORM' WEISS

He is of German descent. He was a Progressive Conservative cabinet minister as of 1990.

ELIABETH 'Beth' WENDORFF

The name would indicate ethnic German descent. Beth Wendoroff unsuccessfully ran as a Liberal for the Cardston Provincial constituency in 1989.

DAVID G. WERESCHUK

Born in 1912. When young, he qualified as a teacher and taught for five years. Later he qualified as a carpenter and went into the construction business. Came to Calgary in 1969, he worked in construction. In the mid-60's he became unemployed. Interested in federal politics, David Wereschuk, running as an Independent, unsuccessfully contested the Calgary East riding in the September 1984 general election. In field of eight candidates, he placed fourth and forfeited his deposit. Conservative Dr. Alex Kindy won the seat. Turning to provincial politics, David Wereschuk, running as an Independent, unsuccessfully contested Calgary Millican in 1986. In a field of five candidates, he placed fourth and again forfeited his deposit.

G. 'Bear' WERSCHLER

The name would indicate ethnic German descent. G. Werschler unsuccessfully ran as a Liberal for the Drayton Valley Provincial constituency in 1989.

POUL WESCH

The name would indicate ethnic German descent. Poul Wesch unsuccessfully ran as a Social Creditor for the Three Hills Provincial Constituency in 1989.

ARTHUR WIEBE

For many years, he was an insurance agent. Interested in federal politics, Arthur Wiebe, running as a Social Crediter, unsuccessfully contested the Acadia riding in the 1965 general election. He placed second, losing to Conservative incumbent Jack Horner by a 3,429-vote margin and forfeited his deposit.

ED WIECLAW

The name would indicate ethnic German descent. He became a Vegreville building inspector before unsuccessfully running as a Liberal for the Vegreville federal riding in 1988.

ED WIESGERBER

He was a resident of Barrhead. Interested in federal politics, Ed Wiesgerber, running as a Social Crediter, unsuccessfully contested the Jasper-Edson riding in the 1965 general election. He placed third and forfeited his deposit.

DAVID WITTIS

Born in 1923 at Calgary, his parents were Russian- German immigrants who came to Alberta in 1907. He was educated at Calgary. During World War II, he enlisted in the Canadian Army and served overseas. While in Britain, he became interested in socialism and became active in labour circles after being demobilized. For a while, he was a Merchant Seaman sailing out of Halifax. On returning to Calgary, he joined the Labor Progressive (Communist) Party. Interested in federal politics, David Wittis unsuccessfully contested the Calgary North riding in 1953. In a filed of five candidates, he placed last and forfeited his deposit. Conservative incumbent Douglas S. Harkness retained the seat. During the campaign, Wittis stated that by slavishly following anti-national policies of selling out the priceless heritage of the nation, the people responsible demonstrated their utter inability to lead the nation forward. He maintained the position that Canada was not simply a piece of real estate to be sold piece meal to the highest bidder.

About the Authors

Ernest George Mardon:

Born in Houston Texas, and is an emeritus professor at the University of Lethbridge. He has published several books on Albertan studies.

Austin Albert Mardon:

He is the first native Albertan to see the Antarctic polar plateau and has been recognized for this accomplishment by the Canadian Senate, the Alberta Legislature, the US Congress, and the Texas State House of Representatives. He has received two decorations for his service in the Antarctic and published over 100 research communications.

Austin A. Mardon & Ernest G. Mardon

Works in Progress.

Introductory Essay to Alberta Political Biographical Dictionary.

What is the Democratic Process?

The Essence of the true democratic process is that individuals are selected from the collective whole of a society to act on behalf of that collective society in the arena of political governance. During the process of governance, we sometimes forget that the representatives that are elected are only part of the democratic arena. Within many societies, the losers do not accept their defeat gently and with grace.

For democracy to continue to exist, these defeated candidates must be willing to accept the will of the people as expressed through the ballot box and selection of candidates. Historically in many societies disintegration of the political process and the transfer of power is instigated by losers in the voting process taking up arms.

Many would ask why the losers would be included in a history of the political landscape of Alberta: it is for the above reason. That these losing candidates are a distinct part of the political process and for our societies' continued smooth functioning it is only with their peaceful acceptance of "the will of the people" that our political institutions continue to exist. The other assumption of our work is that the individual life history of each individual politician distinctly affects the manner in which they chart the course of the state. As Lord Thomas Macauley, the 19th Century British historian, states, "History is ultimately biography." The Marxist historical analyst would question the validity of individual biographies. There would be an attempt to look at broader sweeps of historical action; notwithstanding this attempt, it is only by developing taxonomies of biographies and coherent schemas based on established historical fact that a true comprehension of reality may be approached. The example we have is the eighty-year analysis of the Mormon political influence on Alberta. The discussion up to the publication of this volume is based on scant spotty research, that is based primarily on speculation and not fact. This work is based solely on facts. With the data and interconnections that are contained in many biographies, the future researchers will be able to base their research on established facts.

The value of this work will not occur at one fell swoop, but in dribs and drabs. This book will be out of print and tattered in the collections of interested researchers. Each separate biography is a source of interesting historical material that can otherwise only be located in a bewildering array of archival sources.

After this work is published, it will be possible to examine the plethora of ethnic groups in the migration waves across Alberta and how they impacted on the political process. The ethnic groups each in their own distinct way contributed to the strength of the democratic process by individual participating members having their names put forward for election to legislature or to represent Alberta in The House of Commons in Ottawa. In many cases it was to take a generation or more for political participation to begin to occur, eventually they assimilated as participating groups in the political process. The pattern that seems evident is that a series of failures at the provincial level can eventually lead to success, namely, election to the Legislative Assembly or Parliament.

The characteristics of gender participation are quite disturbing, because women represent the largest minority group in the Province, as far as representation is concerned, yet they have distinctly not had a proportional representation of candidates even up to the present. The female candidates have, however, been spread out, putting themselves forward as candidates over the entire political spectrum.

While errors are bound to exist in any monograph, the

reader should not forget that the purpose of such a work is to see the total pattern of all the candidates. This book is the only work ever done in the Western World that contains all candidates, the winners and the losers; as such might it be the model of other political regional works. In addition, the biographical profiles can be extracted and subdivided by various geographical and ethnic characteristics. The reader hopefully will see the purpose of these brief biographical sketches.

If the reader has encountered any factual errors, please contact the author through the publisher, or if they have any additional material that they feel would add to the depth of any individual biography, please contact the author, again... if the reader has any comments on the above work, please contact:

Dr. E. G. Mardon,

C/O Red Deer College, Box 5005,
Red Deer, Alberta,
T4N 5H1

I Archdeacons Monro's Description of the Western Isles of Scotland: 1549. Translated into Modern English by E.G. Mardon and A.A. Mardon. 1990. Paperback ISBN 1-895385-04-0, $20; Hardcover ISBN 1-895385-06-7, $30.

II Alberta Ethnic Mormon Politicians 1880's- 1990's: A Mormon Contribution to Canadian Democracy. By Dr. E.G. Mardon & A.A. Mardon, with an Introduction by Dr. B.Y. Card. 1990. Paperback ISBN 1-895385-00-8, $20; Hardcover ISBN 1-895385-02-4, $30.

III Alberta Judicial Biographical Dictionary. By Dr. E.G. Mardon & A. A. Mardon. 1990. Paperback ISBN 1-895385-12-1, $20; Hardcover ISBN 1- 895385-14-8, $30.

IV Alberta Ethnic German Politicians. By E.G. Mardon & A.A. Mardon. 1990. Paperback ISBN 1-895385-24-5, $20; Hardcover ISBN 1□895385-26-1, $30.

V The Men of the Dawn: Alberta Political Territorial Biographical Dictionary 1882- 1905. By E.G. Mardon & A.A. Mardon. 1991. Paperback ISBN 1-895385-16-4, $20; Hardcover ISBN 1-895385-22□9, $30.

VI Alberta Executive Council 1905- 1990. 1991. By E.G. Mardon & A.A. Mardon. 1991. Paperback ISBN 1-895385-18-0, $20; Hardcover ISBN 1- 895385-20-2, $30.

Forthcoming Publication is available for free from Alberta Culture and Multiculturalism titled "Alberta Political Biographical Dictionary 1882-1980." Occasional Paper series (1990 date) in three volumes. Address written requests to:

Minister.

Alberta Department of Culture and Multiculturalism.

Legislative Assembly, Edmonton, Alberta, CANADA.

Alberta Ethnic German Politicians

Alberta Ethnic German Politicians

Austin A. Mardon & Ernest G. Mardon

Alberta Ethnic German Politicians

www.ingramcontent.com/pod-product-compliance
Lightning Source LLC
LaVergne TN
LVHW050941080826
845145LV00004B/1350

* 9 7 8 1 8 9 7 4 7 2 2 8 6 *